L-2.3
P-0.5

W9-DGS-763

# All Kinds of People

## What Makes Us Different

by Jennifer Waters

Content and Reading Adviser: Mary Beth Fletcher, Ed.D.
Educational Consultant/Reading Specialist
The Carroll School, Lincoln, Massachusetts

**COMPASS POINT BOOKS**

Minneapolis, Minnesota

Compass Point Books
3722 West 50th Street, #115
Minneapolis, MN 55410

Visit Compass Point Books on the Internet at *www.compasspointbooks.com*
or e-mail your request to *custserv@compasspointbooks.com*

Project Manager: Rebecca Weber McEwen
Editor: Heidi Schoof
Photo Researcher: Image Select International Limited
Photo Selectors: Rebecca Weber McEwen and Heidi Schoof
Designer: Erin Scott, SARIN creative
Illustrator: Anna-Maria Crum


**Library of Congress Cataloging-in-Publication Data**

Waters, Jennifer.
 All kinds of people: what makes us different / by Jennifer Waters.
     p. cm. — (Spyglass books)
Summary: Explores the diversity among humankind, including differences
in physical appearance, communication, mobility, and personality.
Includes bibliographical references and index.
 ISBN 0-7565-0377-9 (hardcover)
 1. Physical anthropology—Juvenile literature. 2. Human anatomy—Variation—
Juvenile literature. [1. Individuality.] I. Title. II. Series.
 GN62.8 .W38 2002
 599.9—dc21
                              2002002539

# Contents

# All Kinds of People

All kinds of people live on this Earth.

No two people are exactly alike—not even twins!

# How People Look

## Hair

There are people with black hair, red hair, brown hair, or blond hair.

Some people have curly hair or straight hair. Some people have no hair at all.

# Skin

There are people with dark skin, with light skin, or with in-between skin.

Some people have smooth skin. Some have *wrinkles*.

9

# Eyes

There are people with brown eyes, with blue eyes, with *hazel* eyes, or with green eyes.

Some people wear glasses.

# Language

There are more than 6,000 *languages* spoken around the world.

Some people speak more than one language. Some people use sign language.

There are people who can move fast and people who move slow.

Some people use a wheelchair. Some people use crutches, a *cane*, or a *walker*.

14

# Personality

There are many kinds of *personalities*. Some people talk a lot. Some people are quiet.

Some people like to play outside. Some like to stay inside and read.

Everybody is different.
This is good.

Life would be *boring* if we did
not know all kinds of people.

# Fun Facts

## Long Mustache

A man named Kalyan Ramji Sain grew a mustache that was 133½ inches (339 cm) long.

## Long Life

A French woman named Jeanne-Louise Calment lived to be 122 years and 164 days old.

## Fast People

Human beings can run as fast as 28 miles (45 kilometers) per hour.

## Tall Man

Robert Wadlow, of Illinois, stood more than 8 feet 11 inches (2 meters 72 centimeters) tall.

# Glossary

*boring*–not fun or exciting

*cane*–a special stick that people lean on to help them walk

*hazel*–a brownish-yellow eye color that can also look blue or green

*language*–the different kinds of words or signals people use to talk to each other

*personality*–the ways each person does things and feels about things that make him or her special

*walker*–a tool that people hold and lean on to help them walk

*wrinkle*–a line or fold people get on their skin as they grow older

# Learn More

## Books

Wood, Jenny. *The Children's Atlas of People and Places*. Brookfield, Conn.: The Millbrook Press, 1993.

Sanders, Pete. *What It's Like to Be Old*. New York: Gloucester Press, 1991.

Green, Jen. *Dealing with Racism*. Brookfield, Conn.: Copper Beech Books, 1997.

## Web Sites

planetspin.luxline.com

snaithprimary.eril.net/diversit.htm

# Index

**GR:  F**

**Word Count:  181**

# From  Jennifer  Waters

I  live   near   the  Rocky  Mountains,
but  the  ocean  is  my  favorite  place.
I  like  to  write  songs  and  books.
I  hope  you  enjoyed  this  book.